The Little
SOCK KNITTING BOOK

Learn the Basics
with Colorful, Stylish Projects

Veronika Hug & Co.

Contents

Sock Knitting Made Easy	4
Knitting with Double-Pointed Needles	5
Anatomy of a Sock	8
Materials and Care	10
Round Cast On	11
Long-Tail Cast On	12
Ribbing	14
Leg Patterns	16
Heel Flap	18
Short-Row (Boomerang) Heel	20
Step Heel	22
Classic Toe (Band Toe)	24
Star Toe	25

30

32

34

2 THE LITTLE SOCK KNITTING BOOK

Propeller Toe	26
Snail Toe	27
Size Chart, 4-Ply Yarn	28
Size Chart, 6-Ply Yarn	29
Sock with Heel Flap	30
Sock with Short-Row Heel	32
Sock with Step Heel	34
Spiral Sock: Knitted from the Toe Up	36
Spiral Sock with Openwork Pattern	38
Toe-Up Sock: The Reverse Sock	40
Toe-Up Sock with Lace Leg	42
Size Chart for Toe-Up Sock	44
Knitting Basics	45

38

36

42

CONTENTS 3

Sock Knitting Made Easy

Knitting socks isn't hard! This book teaches the basics without unnecessary frills.

  It starts with casting on stitches, followed by rib and leg patterns, which can be customized in various ways. Heels and toes can also be knitted in different styles, meaning you can make a unique sock all the way down to the toe.

  Each section of the sock is explained step by step with instructional photos. You can try out the variations before deciding on the method that works best for you. The Knitting Basics section covers different types of stitches and patterns, as well as various increases and decreases.

  Size charts ensure perfectly fitting socks, and the instructions for sample socks let you complete your first projects right away.

  You only need a little to make sock knitting easy and fun!

Knitting with Double-Pointed Needles

Needles

Socks are knitted in rounds using double-pointed needles (DPNs). A DPN set consists of five equally long needles with points on both ends. They are available in sizes ranging from US size 4/0 to 36 (1.25–20mm) and in lengths of 4", 6", and 8" (10.2, 15.2, and 20.3cm). DPNs can be made from aluminum, wood, bamboo, or plastic. A needle gauge tool can help quickly check that all needles in the set are the same size.

Gauge Swatch

Following the gauge is essential to ensure well-fitting socks. The gauge—number of stitches per 4" (10.2cm) width and rows per 4" (10.2cm) height—varies depending on the yarn and is always printed on the yarn label.

To determine the correct needle size, knit a swatch of at least 5" x 5" (12.7 x 12.7cm) in the pattern you plan to use for the sock. Treat the swatch the same way as the finished sock: wash and dry it as you would the final product. Then, use a tape measure to count the number of stitches over 4" (10.2cm) in width and rows over 4" (10.2cm) in height.

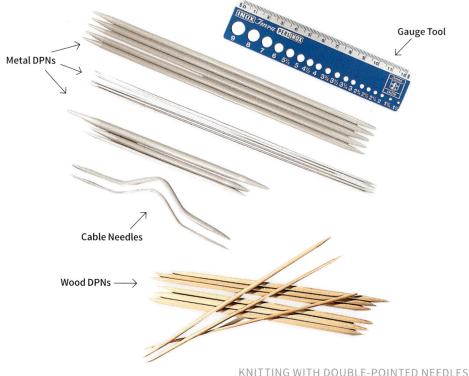

Metal DPNs

Gauge Tool

Cable Needles

Wood DPNs

If your numbers match the gauge on the yarn label, you're ready to start. If you have more stitches than indicated, use thicker needles. If you have fewer stitches, use thinner needles. In either case, knit another swatch and measure again. Having a variety of needle sizes on hand is helpful. The recommended needle size for that particular yarn is also printed on the label.

> **Tips and Tricks**
> When pulling yarn from the skein, it often bounces around. To avoid this, use the yarn end from the center of the skein.
>
> For self-patterning yarns, pay attention to the color sequence. Find the corresponding color point in the yarn for the second sock that matches the starting point of the first sock to ensure both socks look identical. If using two 1.75oz (50g) skeins, determine the starting points for both socks before knitting.

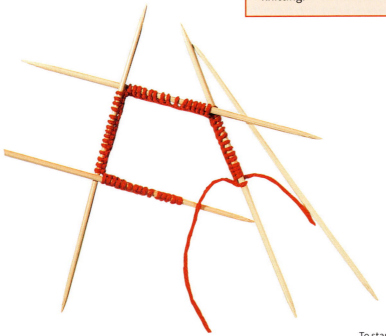

To start your sock project, distribute yarn across four needles.

THE LITTLE SOCK KNITTING BOOK

Needle Arrangement

When casting on, distribute the stitches evenly across four needles of the DPN set and join the stitches in the round (see page 6). To mark the beginning of the round, tie a contrasting thread between needles 1 and 4 or use a stitch marker. Needle 5 is used for knitting.

Knitting in the Round

To join the round, arrange the needles in a square with the lower edges of the stitches facing inward. Ensure no stitches are twisted. Use needle 5 to knit the stitches from needle 1, with the working yarn coming from needle 4. Knit the first few stitches tightly to avoid gaps at the transition.

Tips and Tricks

Small gaps often appear at the shift between needles when knitting in the round. This can be avoided by knitting the first stitch on each needle tightly. Another solution is to periodically redistribute the stitches on the needles, which helps even out irregularities. Before beginning the heel, return the stitches to their original arrangement.

Hand-knitted socks often have smooth soles, which can be slippery on surfaces like tiles, hardwood, and laminate flooring. This is especially a concern for children's socks. Consider adding anti-slip grips to the soles. Premade anti-slip pads in various shapes and colors are available for ironing onto socks. Alternatively, use liquid latex to paint custom grips directly onto the socks. However, socks treated with latex should not be tumble-dried.

KNITTING WITH DOUBLE-POINTED NEEDLES

Anatomy of a Sock

A knitted sock consists of several sections:

The **cast-on edge** forms the cuff's border. Different cast-on methods create different edges. This book covers the standard long-tail cast on and a stretchy variation (pages 12–13), as well as the round cast on (page 11).

Typically knitted in a rib pattern for elasticity, the **cuff** prevents the sock from slipping. Other styles, like picot edges, are also possible. Pages 14–15 explore various cuff designs.

The **leg** begins right after the cuff and is the visible part of the sock when worn with shoes. It can be knitted in simple stockinette, a continuation of the cuff pattern, or decorative designs like lace or cables. Note that cables tighten the fabric, so additional stitches may be needed. The leg transitions into the heel on needles 1 and 4, and into the instep on needles 2 and 3.

The **heel** should fit snugly and look neat. Common heel types include the heel flap, short-row heel, and step heel. Heels are typically knitted flat in rows. Detailed instructions for these styles are on pages 18–23. Reinforcement is recommended, either by adding a strand of reinforcing yarn or using a textured stitch pattern.

The **gusset** joins the heel and instep, reducing stitches to match the foot's circumference.

The **foot** section is between the heel and toe. While large enough for patterns, plain stockinette is preferred for comfort. Refer to the size chart for the required length.

The **toe** covers the front of the foot and can be knitted in various styles. Pages 24–27 explain band, star, propeller, and snail toes.

Most socks are knitted from cuff to toe, but **toe-up socks** are also possible. Instructions and a pattern for toe-up socks are on pages 40–44.

The **spiral sock**, covered on pages 36–39, is unique in that it doesn't require a heel or gusset.

For a Reinforced Heel:

Row 1: Alternate slipping 1 stitch with yarn behind the work and knitting 1 stitch.

Row 2: Knit stitches as they appear.

Row 3: Repeat Row 1, shifting the pattern by 1 stitch.

Row 4: Knit stitches as they appear.

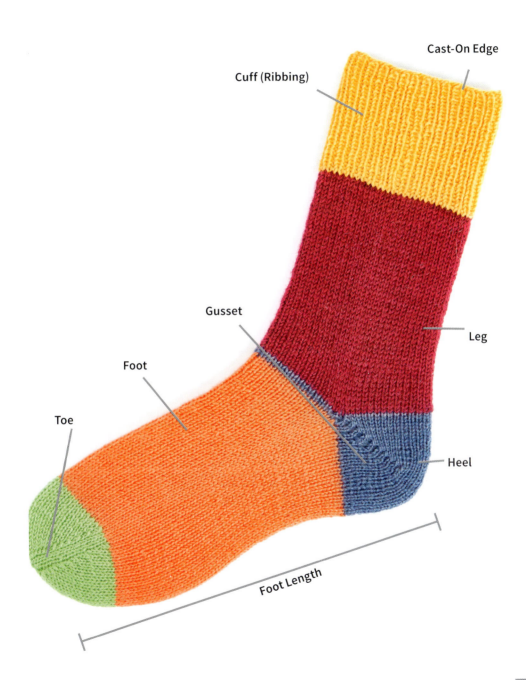

ANATOMY OF A SOCK

Materials and Care

Socks made from pure wool are not very durable. Many yarn manufacturers offer special sock yarns blended with other fibers to withstand wear and tear better. These yarns often feature a "superwash" treatment, making them machine washable.

Blends of wool, nylon, and acrylic are suitable for warm, durable socks. For lighter socks, cotton-wool-nylon blends are recommended. These should be knitted tightly for an even texture.

Yarn blends with silk, bamboo, or stretch fibers are also available. Silk adds a slight sheen and enhances stitch definition.

Bamboo provides comfort and a smooth finish, making patterns stand out. Bamboo yarn is best knitted tightly but is slippery on metal needles. Stretch fibers ensure a snug fit. To maintain this property, avoid knitting the yarn too tightly.

The trend toward natural fibers has introduced sock yarns with ramie, a tropical plant fiber that adds shine and durability.

Sock yarn comes in various weights. The most common is **4-ply yarn**. Made of four twisted strands, it provides warmth without being too thick, allowing for detailed patterns. One 1.75oz (50g) skein is sufficient for socks up to Men's size 13.

The ideal option for thicker, warmer socks is **6-ply yarn**. However, socks with patterns may feel tight in shoes. Approximately 5.25oz (150g) are needed for a pair.

For intricate patterns or lighter socks, use **3-ply yarn**. About 2.75oz (78g) is needed for a pair.

Some yarns include a small spool of **2-ply reinforcing yarn**, often hidden inside the skein, for strengthening the heel. Reinforcing yarn is also available separately in various colors.

Sock yarn comes in a wide range of colors and patterns, from self-striping and gradients to solid colors. The variety continues to grow, enhancing both the knitting process and the final product's appeal.

Self-patterning yarns add a bit of flair to custom socks, but don't discount the beauty of a solid color!

THE LITTLE SOCK KNITTING BOOK

Round Cast On

1. Casting on with Waste Yarn: Use a larger needle size than usual and a contrasting color yarn to cast on half the required number of stitches. Then, switch to a smaller needle size and the working yarn (e.g., yellow).

Round 1: Work 1 knit stitch, 1 yarn over alternately while distributing stitches across four needles and joining in the round.

Round 2: Slip the knit stitches purlwise with the yarn in the back. Purl the yarn overs.

Round 3: Knit all knit stitches. Slip the purl stitches purlwise with the yarn in front.

Round 4: Repeat Round 2: slip knit stitches with yarn in the back, purl the purl stitches.

Switch to the standard needle size and knit the ribbing in 2 knit stitches, 2 purl stitches.

2. Removing the Waste Yarn: After a few rows, cut the waste yarn every 3–4 stitches and remove it.

3. Finishing: The completed ribbing will have a neat, rounded edge.

Long-Tail Cast On

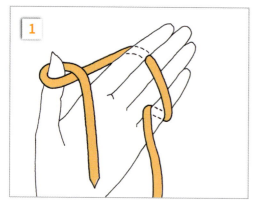

1. Measuring the Tail: For medium-weight yarns, allow about ¾" (1.9cm) of yarn per stitch, slightly less for thinner yarns, plus an additional 7 ¾" (19.7cm). For 4-ply yarn and 64 stitches, approximately 47" (119.4cm) is required. Wrap the yarn end around your left pinky finger, pass it between your index and middle fingers to the back, then forward over your index finger. Wrap it from front to back around your thumb.

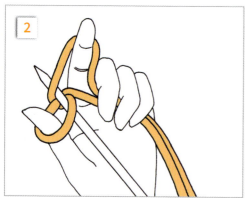

2. Inserting the Needle: Hold both ends of the yarn firmly. Insert the right needle upward into the loop around your thumb. Pass the right needle behind the yarn coming from your index finger . . .

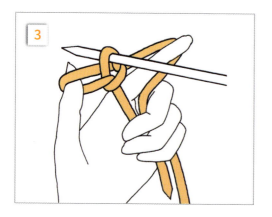

3. Pulling the Yarn Through: . . . and pull this yarn through the loop on your thumb. Let the loop slide off your thumb.

THE LITTLE SOCK KNITTING BOOK

4. Tightening the Stitch: Use your thumb to grab the tail yarn from back to front. Tighten the stitch and raise your thumb.

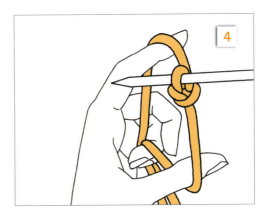

5. Forming the First Stitch: The first stitch is now on the right needle. Insert the needle into the loop around your thumb again, pull the yarn through, and tighten the loop.

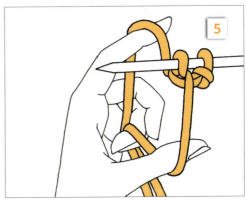

6. Repeating for More Stitches: Each repetition of this process forms a new stitch.

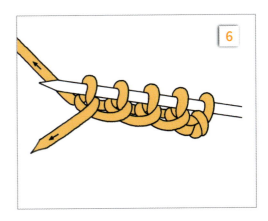

LONG-TAIL CAST ON

Ribbing

1x1 Ribbing:

Requires an even number of stitches. Cast on the desired number of stitches and alternate 1 knit stitch, 1 purl stitch. This ribbing is very elastic and pairs well with many patterns.

2x2 Ribbing:

Requires a multiple of 4 stitches. Cast on the desired number of stitches and alternate 2 knit stitches, 2 purl stitches. This ribbing is also elastic and complements various patterns.

Rolled Edge

Cast on the desired number of stitches and knit all stitches for about 1"–1 ½" (2.5–3.8cm). The edge will roll up naturally. This edge is not very elastic but can be paired with ribbing to address this.

Picot Edge

Cast on an even number of stitches very loosely. Knit 1 ½" (3.8cm) in stockinette. For the fold line: *knit 2 stitches together, yarn over, repeat from * to the end of the round. Knit another 1 ½" (3.8cm) in stockinette. Using a thinner needle, pick up 1 stitch from each cast-on stitch. Hold the needles parallel and knit 1 stitch from the front needle together with 1 from the back needle to join.

Crochet Edge

Work a crochet border along the cast-on edge, inserting the crochet hook only into the purl bumps of the cast-on edge in the first round.

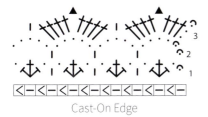

Cast-On Edge

Legend on page 32

Small Cables

Requires a stitch count divisible by 3. Cast on the required number of stitches. **Round 1:** Work 1 purl stitch, 2 knit stitches. **Round 2:** Work 1 purl stitch, place 1 stitch on a cable needle held at the front, knit 1 stitch, then knit the stitch from the cable needle. Repeat Rounds 1 and 2 until the ribbing reaches the desired height.

RIBBING 15

Leg Patterns

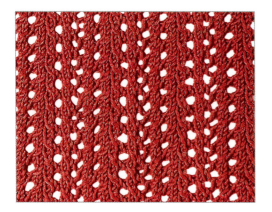

Openwork Pattern

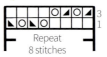

Repeat 8 stitches

Legend

☐ = K
◤ = K2tog
◣ = SKP
O = YO

In the even rounds (intermediate rounds), knit all stitches and yarn overs.

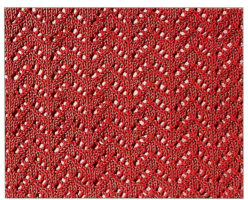

Openwork Arrows

Repeat 8 stitches

Legend

☐ = K
◤ = K2tog
◣ = SKP
↑ = SK2P
O = YO

In the even rounds (intermediate rounds), knit all stitches and yarn overs.

Openwork Pattern

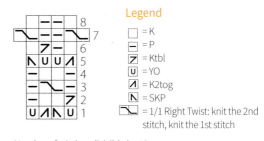

Legend

☐ = K
— = P
⌐ = Ktbl
U = YO
◤ = K2tog
◣ = SKP
⌒ = 1/1 Right Twist: knit the 2nd stitch, knit the 1st stitch

Number of stitches divisible by 12.

Texture Pattern

Repeat 8 stitches

Legend

 = K
 = P

Texture Pattern

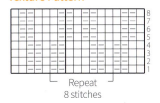

Repeat 8 stitches

Legend

□ = K
⊟ = P

Cable Pattern

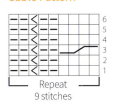

Repeat 9 stitches

Legend

□ = K
⊟ = P
 = Ktbl
= 2/2 Right Cross: place 2 stitches on the cable needle in back, K2, K2 on the cable

LEG PATTERNS 17

Heel Flap

1. Heel Flap: Transfer the stitches from needles 1 and 4 onto one needle and knit in stockinette stitch (knit on right-side rows, purl on wrong-side rows). Optionally, work the two outermost stitches in garter stitch (knit both on right- and wrong-side rows). The stitches from needles 2 and 3 are placed on hold. Refer to the size chart for the number of rows needed for the heel flap.

2. Heel Turn: Divide the stitches of the heel flap into three equal parts. Work in stockinette stitch over the middle third, gradually incorporating stitches from the outer thirds as described in step 3.

Note: The heel shown here is worked in a reinforced pattern (refer to instructions on page 8).

3. Shaping the Heel:
  On right-side rows: Knit the last stitch of the middle third together with the first stitch of the left outer third through the back loop. To do this, insert the needle from the back through both stitches, yarn over, pull the yarn through, and drop the stitches from the needle. Turn the work and slip the first stitch purlwise on the wrong side.
  On wrong-side rows: Purl the last stitch of the middle third together with the first stitch of the outer third. Turn the work and slip the first stitch knitwise.

4. Continuing the Heel Turn: Repeat step 3 until all stitches from the outer thirds are used up, leaving only the stitches from the middle third on the needle.

5. Rejoining in the Round: Resume knitting in the round on four needles. Divide the heel stitches evenly onto needles 1 and 4. Pick up 1 stitch from every other row along the left edge of the heel flap with needle 1, and do the same along the right edge with needle 4.

6. Shaping the Gusset: In every second round, decrease the extra stitches as follows:

On needle 1: Knit the third-to-last and second-to-last stitches together.

On needle 4: Slip the second stitch knitwise, knit the third stitch, then pass the slipped stitch over.

Repeat these decreases until needles 1 and 4 have the same number of stitches as at the start of the heel. Continue knitting the foot according to the size chart until the required foot length is reached.

HEEL FLAP

Short-Row (Boomerang) Heel

1. Preparation: The boomerang heel is worked over half the total stitches, i.e., the stitches on needles 1 and 4. Divide these stitches into three parts. Place the stitches from needles 2 and 3 on hold.

2. First Half of the Heel:
Row 1 (right-side row): Knit all stitches on needle 1, then turn the work.
Row 2 (wrong-side row): Create a double stitch by bringing the yarn to the front, inserting the needle from right to left into the first stitch, slipping it along with the yarn, and pulling the yarn firmly to the back (this prevents holes). The stitch will appear doubled.
Bring the yarn forward again and purl the remaining stitches on needle 1 and all stitches on needle 4. Turn the work.

3. Continue:
Row 3 (right-side row): Create a double stitch at the start of the row. Knit across needles 4 and 1 up to the last double stitch, leaving it unworked. Turn the work.
Row 4 (wrong-side row): Create a double stitch at the start of the row. Purl across needle 1 and needle 4 up to the last double stitch, leaving it unworked. Turn the work.

4. Repeat **Rows 3 and 4** until only the stitches of the middle third minus two stitches remain between the double stitches. Then knit two rounds across all stitches on needles 1–4, knitting the double stitches as one stitch in the first round.

5. Second Half of the Heel:
   Row 1 (right-side row): Knit the stitches from the first and middle thirds. Turn the work.
   Row 2 (wrong-side row): Create a double stitch and purl the stitches of the middle third. Turn the work.
   Row 3 (right-side row): Create a double stitch, knit to the double stitch, knit it as described, knit the next stitch, then turn the work.
   Row 4 (wrong-side row): Create a double stitch, purl to the double stitch, purl it as described, purl the next stitch, then turn the work.

6. Continue repeating **Rows 3 and 4** until all heel stitches are worked again. Resume knitting in the round and continue until the required foot length is reached.

SHORT-ROW (BOOMERANG) HEEL

Step Heel

1. Combine the stitches from needles 1 and 4 onto one needle and work in rows. Place the stitches from needles 2 and 3 on hold. The step heel can be knitted in stockinette stitch (knit right-side rows, purl wrong-side rows) or reinforced (see page 8).

2. Knit the two outermost stitches of the heel in garter stitch (knit both right- and wrong-side rows) to make counting rows easier and for a more pronounced edge. Knit the number of rows specified in the size chart for the first step. Once this number of rows is reached, place the last stitches (as indicated in the size chart) on hold at the end of the next row. In the following wrong-side row, place the same number of stitches on hold at the end of the row.

3. Continue working in stockinette stitch or reinforced pattern over the remaining stitches, keeping the two outermost stitches in garter stitch. Work the number of rows specified in the size chart for the second step. At the end of the next row, pick up one stitch from the edge for every two rows along the edge of the first step.

THE LITTLE SOCK KNITTING BOOK

4. Incorporate the held stitches back into the heel. In every second row, knit the first stitch of the held stitches together with the last stitch of the heel, passing the heel stitch over. Turn the work, slip the first stitch purlwise, purl the remaining stitches, and pick up the same number of stitches from the opposite edge as were picked up previously. Knit the last-picked-up stitch together with the first stitch of the held stitches on the wrong side.

Continue in stockinette or reinforced stitch, slipping the first stitch of each row and knitting the last stitch together with the first stitch of the held stitches on the right side, or purling together on the wrong side. Repeat until all held stitches are worked back into the heel. The row count is also noted in the size chart. After finishing, slip the first stitch and knit half of the stitches (these will become the stitches for needle 4).

5. Divide the stitches onto 4 needles as follows: Place the second half of the heel stitches onto needle 1. Pick up 1 stitch from every two rows along the left edge of the first step using needle 1 (as indicated for gusset stitches in the size chart).

Resume knitting the held stitches from needles 2 and 3. Pick up 1 stitch from every two rows along the right edge of the first step using needle 4 and finish knitting the remaining heel stitches onto needle 4.

6. To shape the gusset, decrease stitches in every second round: On needle 1, knit the third-to-last and second-to-last stitches together. On needle 4, slip the second stitch knitwise, knit the third stitch, then pass the slipped stitch over.

Repeat until needles 1 and 4 have the same number of stitches as needles 2 and 3. Continue knitting the foot to the desired length.

STEP HEEL

Classic Toe (Band Toe)

1. The band toe is the classic among sock toes. In every second round, decrease as follows:

On needles 1 and 3, knit the second-to-last and third-to-last stitches together.

On needles 2 and 4, slip the second stitch knitwise, knit the third stitch, and pass the slipped stitch over.

2. When 8–12 stitches remain, pull the yarn tightly through all stitches twice and weave in the end on the inside.

3. The band toe is simple to knit, but some wearers find the "bands" at the front of the sock uncomfortable.

Star Toe

1. Ensure each needle has an even number of stitches before starting. Distribute extra stitches evenly in the preceding rounds if needed. On each needle, work 2 decreases according to the star toe number from the size chart. This number indicates how many rounds to knit before the first decrease round.

2. For example, with a star toe number of 7: Knit 6 rounds without decreases.

On Round 7, knit every sixth and seventh stitch together. The number of stitches between decreases determines how many rounds are worked without decreases. In this case, 5 stitches remain between decreases, so knit 5 rounds without decreases.

3. Repeat the process, decreasing the gap between decreases and the number of rounds without decreases, until only 2 stitches remain on each needle (8 stitches total). Pull the yarn tightly through all stitches twice and weave in the end.

The star toe has a symmetrical appearance and doesn't press against the toes.

Propeller Toe

1. Decreases in Every Second Round: Knit the first and second stitches on each needle together. Continue decreasing in this manner in every second round.

2. Switch to Every Round: When only one-third of the original number of stitches remains, switch to decreasing in every round.

3. Finish the Toe: Continue until only 2 stitches remain on each needle (8 stitches total). Pull the yarn tightly through all remaining stitches twice and secure the end on the inside of the sock.

The propeller-like pattern of the decreases gives this toe its name. This shape is ideal for pointed feet.

Snail Toe

1. Decreases in Every Second Round: On each needle, work a decrease by slipping the second stitch knitwise, knitting the third stitch, and passing the slipped stitch over.

2. Continue Until Few Stitches Remain: Repeat the decrease rounds until only 2 stitches remain on each needle (8 stitches total).

3. Secure the Toe: Pull the yarn tightly through all remaining stitches twice and weave in the end on the inside of the sock. The spiral formed by the emphasized decreases gives the snail toe its name. This durable toe is comfortable to wear and fits well in shoes.

Size Chart, 4-Ply Yarn

US Size (EU Size)	Kids' 8 (24)	Kids' 9.5 (26)	Kids' 11.5 (29)	Kids' 12.5 (30)	Kids' 1.5 (33)	Women's 5 (35/36)	Women's 6.5 (37)	Women's 8 (38/39)	Women's 9.5 (40)	Men's 9.5 (42/43)	Men's 11 (44)	Men's 13 (46)	Men's 14 (47)
Foot length in inches (cm)	5 ¾" (14.6cm)	6 ¼" (15.9cm)	7" (17.8cm)	7 ¼" (18.4cm)	8" (20.3cm)	8 ½" (21.6cm)	9" (22.9cm)	9 ½" (24.1cm)	10" (25.4cm)	10 ½" (26.7cm)	11" (27.9cm)	11 ½" (29.2cm)	12" (30.5cm)
Number of cast-on stitches	44	48	48	52	52	56	56	60	60	64	64	68	72
Heel Flap													
Heel flap width	22	24	24	26	26	28	28	30	30	32	32	34	36
Heel flap height in rows	20	22	22	24	24	26	26	28	28	30	30	32	34
Number of stitches for the heel turn	8	8	8	8	8	10	10	10	10	10	10	12	12
Stitches picked up on both sides	11	12	12	13	13	14	14	15	15	16	16	17	18
Short-Row Heel (Boomerang Heel)													
Short-row heel (boomerang heel)	7 / 8 / 7	8 / 8 / 8	8 / 8 / 8	8 / 10 / 8	8 / 10 / 8	9 / 10 / 9	9 / 10 / 9	10 / 10 / 10	10 / 10 / 10	10 / 12 / 10	10 / 12 / 10	11 / 12 / 11	12 / 12 / 12
Step Heel													
Heel flap width	22	24	24	26	26	28	28	30	30	32	32	34	36
Rows to first step	8	10	10	12	12	14	14	16	16	18	18	20	22
Stitches held on both sides	3	4	4	5	5	6	6	7	7	8	8	9	10
Rows to second step	6	8	8	10	10	12	12	16	16	18	18	20	22
Stitches picked up on both sides	3	4	4	5	5	6	6	8	8	9	9	10	11
Rows to heel end	6	8	8	10	10	12	12	14	14	16	16	18	20
Gusset stitches picked up on both sides	4	5	5	6	6	7	7	8	8	9	9	10	11
Foot length in inches (cm) from heel center to start of toe shaping	4 ⅓" (11cm)	4 ¾" (12.1cm)	5 ⅓" (13.5cm)	5 ¾" (14.6cm)	6 ¼" (15.9cm)	6 ¾" (17.1cm)	7 ⅛" (18.1cm)	7 ½" (19.1cm)	8 ⅛" (20.6cm)	8 ¼" (21cm)	8 ⅞" (22.5cm)	9 ½" (24.1cm)	9 ⅔" (24.6cm)
Star toe stitch count	5	6	6	6	6	7	7	7	7	8	8	8	9

Size Chart, 6-Ply Yarn

US Size (EU Size)	Kids' 8 (24)	Kids' 9.5 (26)	Kids' 11.5 (29)	Kids' 12.5 (30)	Kids' 1.5 (33)	Women's 5 (35/36)	Women's 6.5 (37)	Women's 8 (38/39)	Women's 9.5 (40)	Men's 9.5 (42/43)	Men's 11 (44)	Men's 13 (46)	Men's 14 (47)
Foot length in inches (cm)	5 ¾" (14.6cm)	6 ¼" (15.9cm)	7" (17.8cm)	7 ¼" (18.4cm)	8" (20.3cm)	8 ½" (21.6cm)	9" (22.9cm)	9 ½" (24.1cm)	10" (25.4cm)	10 ½" (26.7cm)	11" (27.9cm)	11 ½" (29.2cm)	12" (30.5cm)
Number of cast-on stitches	32	36	36	40	40	44	44	48	48	52	52	56	56
Heel Flap													
Heel flap width	16	18	18	20	20	22	22	24	24	26	26	28	28
Heel flap height in rows	14	16	16	18	18	20	20	22	22	24	24	26	26
Number of stitches for the heel turn	6	6	6	8	8	8	8	8	8	10	10	10	10
Stitches picked up on both sides	9	10	11	11	12	12	13	14	14	15	15	16	16
Short-Row Heel (Boomerang Heel)													
Short-row heel (boomerang heel)	5 / 6 / 5	6 / 6 / 6	6 / 6 / 6	6 / 8 / 6	6 / 8 / 6	7 / 8 / 7	7 / 8 / 7	8 / 8 / 8	8 / 8 / 8	8 / 10 / 12	8 / 10 / 12	9 / 10 / 9	9 / 10 / 9
Step Heel													
Heel flap width	16	18	18	20	20	22	22	24	24	26	26	28	28
Rows to first step	6	8	8	8	10	10	10	12	12	14	14	16	16
Stitches held on both sides	2	3	3	4	4	5	5	5	5	6	6	7	7
Rows to second step	4	6	6	8	8	10	10	10	10	12	12	14	14
Stitches picked up on both sides	2	3	3	4	4	5	5	5	5	6	6	7	7
Rows to heel end	4	6	6	8	8	10	10	10	10	12	12	14	14
Gusset stitches picked up on both sides	3	4	4	4	5	5	5	6	6	7	7	8	8
Foot length in inches (cm) from heel center to start of toe shaping	4 ⅓" (11cm)	4 ¾" (12.1cm)	5 ⅓" (13.5cm)	5 ¾" (14.6cm)	6 ¼" (15.9cm)	6 ¾" (17.1cm)	7 ⅛" (18.1cm)	7 ½" (19.1cm)	8 ⅛" (20.6cm)	8 ¼" (21cm)	8 ⅞" (22.5cm)	9 ½" (24.1cm)	9 ⅔" (24.6cm)
Star toe stitch count	5	6	6	6	6	7	7	7	7	8	8	8	9

Sock with Heel Flap

Materials:
- 4-ply sock yarn (75% wool, 25% nylon; 230 yds [210.3m]/1.75oz [50g]): 1.75oz (50g) each in petrol, jade, and off-white
- US size 1 ½ (2.5mm) DPNs

Size: US Men's 9.5 (EU 42/43)
Rib Pattern: Knit 2, purl 2 in the round.

Instructions:
Cast on 64 stitches in petrol, divide evenly onto 4 needles (16 stitches per needle), and join in the round, being careful not to twist.
Cuff: Work 16 rounds in the rib pattern.
Leg: Work 39 rounds in stockinette stitch (knit every round), following the pattern chart (repeat the four-stitch motif as indicated).

When switching colors, carry the unused yarn loosely along the back of your work.
Heel: Continue in petrol and work the heel flap as described on pages 18–19.
Foot: Work the foot in stockinette for 8 ¼" (21cm), measured from the middle of the heel.
Toe: Finish the sock by working the toe as described on page 24.

Pattern Chart

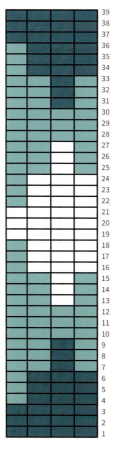

Legend

■ = K in petrol
■ = K in turquoise
□ = K in off-white

Knit Rounds 1–39 once.

30 THE LITTLE SOCK KNITTING BOOK

Sock with Short-Row Heel

Materials:
- 4-ply sock yarn (75% wool, 25% nylon; 460 yds [420.6m]/3.5oz [100g]): 3.5oz (100g) in variegated violet and 3.5oz (100g) in pink
- US size 1 ½ (2.5mm) DPNs
- US size B-1 (2.25mm) crochet hook

Size: US Women's 9.5 (EU 40) or Men's 9.5 (EU 42/43)

Stripe Pattern: Multiple of 4 stitches. Follow the chart in rounds.
Each needle will have 4 pattern repeats. Repeat Rounds 1–16 in the given color sequence.

Stockinette Stitch: Knit all stitches in the round.

Crochet Edge: Work the edging along the cast-on edge following the crochet pattern. Begin with the stitches before the pattern repeat, repeat the motif 7 times, and close each round with a slip stitch.

Instructions:
Cast on 64 stitches in variegated violet. Divide evenly onto 4 needles (16 stitches per needle) and join in the round.

Leg: Knit 7" (17.8cm) or 69 rounds in the stripe pattern. End the leg with 5 rounds in variegated violet.

Heel: Work the short-row heel over the 32 stitches on needles 1 and 4 in variegated violet (see pages 20–21).

Continue the stripe pattern over the instep (needles 2 and 3) during the heel.

In the final round of the heel, knit the first 2 stitches on needle 2 together to maintain symmetry in the instep pattern.

Foot: Continue in variegated violet for the sole (32 stitches, needles 1 and 4).

Crochet Pattern

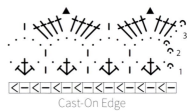

Cast-On Edge

Legend
- · = Chain stitch
- ⌒ = Slip stitch
- | = Single crochet
- ⚓ = Half double crochet + double crochet + half double crochet in a stitch point
- † = Double crochet
- ▲ = Picot: 3 chain stitches and 1 single crochet in the 1st chain stitch

Knitting Pattern

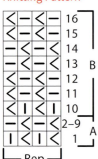

Legend
- **I** = K
- **−** = P
- **<** = Ktbl
- **Rep** = Repeat pattern
- **A** = Variegated violet
- **B** = Pink

For the instep (31 stitches, needles 2 and 3), work the stripe pattern, using Rounds 2–9 of the knitting pattern.

Begin and end the instep pattern with 1 purl stitch.

Work the foot until it measures 7 ¾"–8 ¼" (19.7–21cm) from the heel center.

Toe: In the first round, increase 1 stitch at the start of needle 2 by knitting into the front and back of the same stitch (16 stitches per needle).

Work the toe in pink using the banded toe method (page 24).

Finishing: Add the crochet edge in pink along the cast-on edge, as described on page 15.

In the first round, insert the crochet hook only into the purl bumps of the cast-on edge.

Sock with Step Heel

Materials:
- 4-ply sock yarn (55% merino wool, 20% silk, 25% nylon; 218 yds [199.3m]/1.75oz [50g]): 3.5oz (100g) yellow
- US size 0 (2mm) and size 1 ½ (2.5mm) DPNs
- US size B-1 (2.25mm) crochet hook
- 30 yellow transparent seed beads, 4mm

Size: US Women's 9.5 (EU 40)

Stockinette Stitch (flat): Knit the right-side rows and purl the wrong-side rows.
Stockinette Stitch (in the round): Knit every round.
Rib Pattern: Knit 1, purl 1 in the round.
Lace Pattern: Multiple of 12 stitches. Work according to the chart. Repeat the motif and Rounds 1–8 throughout.

Instructions:

Cuff: Cast on 60 stitches using size 0 (2mm) needles. Divide evenly onto 4 needles (15 stitches per needle) and join in the round.

Knit 6 rounds in stockinette for a small, rolled edge.

Work 5 rounds in rib pattern.

Leg: Switch to size 1 ½ (2.5mm) needles and work the lace pattern according to the chart.

After 2 ⅓" (5.9cm) from the cuff, work the reinforced step heel as described on pages 22–23.

Foot: Knit the stitches on needles 1 and 4, plus the first stitch on needle 2 and the last stitch on needle 3, in stockinette stitch.

Work the middle 28 stitches (on needles 2 and 3) in the lace pattern.

Toe: After 8" (20.3cm) of foot length, work the banded toe in stockinette (see page 24).

Crochet Edge: Thread 15 seed beads onto a long length of sock yarn.

Insert the crochet hook at the level of the last ribbing round, pull the yarn through, and crochet as follows:

Chain 5, incorporate 1 bead, chain 5, skip approximately 4 stitches along the cuff, and secure with 1 single crochet. Repeat until the round is complete.

Knitting Pattern

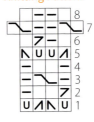

Legend

☐ = K

− = P

𝟋 = Ktbl

U = YO

⋀ = K2tog

⋈ = SKP

⌇ = 1/1 Right Twist: knit the 2nd stitch, knit the 1st stitch

Spiral Sock: Knitted from the Toe Up

Stockinette Stitch (in the round): Knit every round.
Reverse Stockinette Stitch (in the round): Purl every round.

Instructions:
Toe: Cast on 8 stitches across 3 needles, join in the round, and knit 1 round in stockinette.

Increase rounds: **Round 2:** Work a left lifted increase in every stitch (16 stitches total).

Round 4: Increase every second stitch (24 stitches total). **Round 7:** Increase every third stitch (32 stitches total). Distribute stitches onto 4 needles (8 stitches per needle). Continue following the chart for Toe-Up Spiral Pattern 1 until the desired number of stitches is reached.

Spiral Pattern: Knit 2 additional rounds in stockinette. Work Spiral Pattern 2 according to the chart, ensuring the stitch count is divisible by 8 (each motif is 8 stitches). Shift the right and left stitches by 1 stitch to the left every fourth round to create the spiral effect. Repeat Rounds 1–32 of the pattern as needed.

Leg: After reaching ankle height (foot length + heel height), switch to a different leg pattern if desired (e.g., lace). Continue until the leg reaches the desired length, then bind off.

Bind Off: For a stretchy edge, wrap the yarn around the needle before each second stitch. Before purl stitches: Wrap the yarn over the top of the needle from back to front. Before knit stitches: Wrap the yarn under the needle from front to back. Bind off each stitch together with the wrap to create a uniform and elastic edge.

Knitting Chart 1: Increases

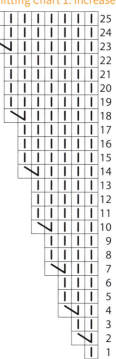

Knitting Chart 2: Basic Pattern

Pattern	Rows
I – – – – I I I	29–32
I I – – – – I I	25–28
I I I – – – – I	21–24
I I I I – – – –	17–20
– I I I I – – –	13–16
– – I I I I – –	9–12
– – – I I I I –	5–8
– – – – I I I I	1–4

Rep

Legend

- I = K
- – = P
- ↘ = LLI
- **Rep** = Repeat pattern

Size Chart, 4-Ply

Gauge stockinette stitch with US size 1 ½–2 ½ (2.5–3mm) DPNs: 28 stitches and 38 rows = 4" x 4" (10.2 x 10.2cm); Cast on 8 stitches

US Size (EU Size)	Number of stitches required	Length from toe, inches (cm)
Baby	32	4 ¾"–6" (12.1–15.2cm)
Kids' 5.5–9.5 (21–26)	40	6"–9" (15.2–22.9cm)
Kids' 10–1 (27–32)	48	8"–11" (20.3–27.9cm)
Kids' 1.5–6.5 (33–38)	56	9 ¾"–12" (24.8–33cm)
Women's 8–12 (39–43)	56–64	11 ¾"–15" (29.8–38.1cm)
Men's 10.5–16 (44–49)	64–72	13 ¾"–17" (34.9–43.2cm)

SPIRAL SOCK: KNITTED FROM THE TOE UP

Spiral Sock with Openwork Pattern

Materials:

- 4-ply sock yarn (75% wool, 25% nylon; 460 yds [420.6m]/3.5oz [100g]): 3.5oz (100g) neon orange
- US size 1 ½ (2.5mm) DPNs

Size: US Women's 9.5–12 (EU 40–43) or Men's 7–11 (EU 40–44)

Rib Pattern: Knit 2, purl 2 in the round.
Basic Pattern: See Chart 2, page 37.
Openwork Pattern: Multiple of 8 stitches. Work the openwork pattern in rounds as per the chart. Always repeat the pattern (Rep). In Rounds 1–12, shift the pattern by 1 stitch to the left every fourth round as shown in the chart.

Instructions:
Cast On and Setup: Cast on 8 stitches, join in the round, and increase to 64 stitches as described on page 36. Continue working in the basic pattern, creating 8 motif repeats.
Leg and Lace Pattern: After 8 ¼" (21cm) or 80 rounds of the basic pattern, continue in the openwork pattern. Adjust the openwork pattern so that the 4 knit stitches meet the previous knit stitches from the basic pattern, shifted by 1 stitch to the left. This should result in 8 motif repeats. After 3 ¾" (9.5cm) or 36 rounds of the openwork pattern, knit ½" (1.3cm) in the rib pattern to finish the leg.
Bind Off: Bind off loosely as shown on page 37.

Legend

I	=	K
—	=	P
U	=	YO
↓	=	SKP
Rep	=	Repeat pattern

Knitting Chart: Openwork Pattern

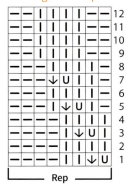

38 THE LITTLE SOCK KNITTING BOOK

Toe-Up Sock: The Reverse Sock

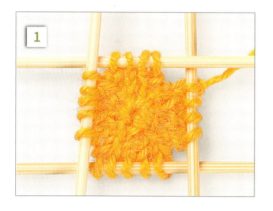

1. Toe: Cast on 6 stitches (this is the same for all sizes). Knit 1 round in stockinette.

Distribute stitches across 3 needles and join in the round. In the next round, increase by 1 stitch in each stitch (12 stitches total). Knit another round, and in the next round, increase every second stitch (18 stitches total). Distribute the stitches onto 4 needles.

2. The stitches will be arranged as follows: Needle 1: First right center stitch, next 7 stitches = top of the foot. Needle 2: 2 left center stitches. Needle 3: 7 stitches = sole. Needle 4: Second right center stitch. Mark the start of the round with a contrasting yarn.

Toe Expansion: In every second round, work a right lifted increase after the 2 center stitches, and a left lifted increase before the 2 center stitches. Repeat this for the required number of increases as indicated in the table.

3. The stitches from needles 1 to 2 form the top of the foot, and the remaining stitches form the sole. Continue knitting for the required number of rounds or inches, as indicated in the table.

For the instep and heel, continue increasing by 1 left lifted increase after the center stitches and 1 right lifted increase before the center stitches, repeating this as indicated in the table.

4. Heel Cap: For the heel cap, continue working over the middle sole stitches on needles 3 and 4 in back-and-forth rows, as specified in the table. On either side of the heel cap, you'll have the heel stitches. Work the first few stitches of the foot back and sole in the round, and knit the last heel-cap stitch together with the first left-heel stitch.

Turn the work, and leave the first stitch unknit, with the yarn in front of the work.

Continue working the remaining stitches of the heel cap in back-and-forth rows, knitting the last stitch of the heel cap together with the following right-heel stitch.

5. Finish Heel Cap: Turn the work, and again leave the first stitch unknit, with the yarn behind the work. Continue knitting the heel-cap stitches and knit the last stitch together with the following left-sole stitch. Repeat the process as indicated in the table on page 44.

6. Leg Completion: After completing the heel cap, continue working in the round, joining the last heel-cap stitch with the next stitch over, as shown in the chart. When the desired leg length is reached, bind off loosely as shown on page 37.

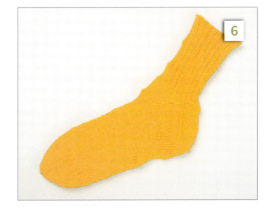

TOE-UP SOCK: THE REVERSE SOCK 41

Toe-Up Sock with Lace Leg

Materials:
- 4-ply sock yarn (75% wool, 25% nylon; 460 yds [420.6m]/3.5oz [100g]): 3.5oz (100g) in Limone
- US size 1 ½ (2.5mm) DPNs

Size: US Women's 9.5 (EU 40) [US Men's 9.5 (EU 42/43)]

Stockinette Stitch (in the round): Knit all stitches. Stockinette (in rows): Knit the right side, purl the wrong side. Stockinette Stitch (in the round, left stitches): Knit all stitches.
Lace Pattern. The number of stitches must be divisible by 8. Follow the knitting chart. Only the odd-numbered rounds are shown; on even rounds, knit all stitches.

When making two consecutive yarn overs, knit the first yarn over normally and work the second one twisted (either right or left). Repeat Rounds 1–12.
Rib Pattern: Knit 1, purl 1 in the round.

Instructions:
Toe: Cast on 6 stitches and increase to 18 stitches as described on page 40. Work in stockinette.
Toe Expansion: Increase 4 stitches on each side of the two center stitches as follows: In every second round, increase 4 stitches. After 7 ½" [8"] (19.1 [20.3cm]), you should have 58 [62] stitches.
Instep and Heel: After reaching 58 [62] stitches, continue to increase for the instep and heel as described on page 41. Work the heel cap over the middle 18 [20] stitches of the sole stitches. On either side, decrease the last or first heel stitch together with a side sole stitch 14 times [18 times]. After the heel cap is completed, you should have 58 stitches left. Continue working in stockinette for the leg.
Leg and Lace Cuff: In the first round after the heel, over the last stitch of the heel cap, work a yarn over and knit the first stitch of the heel together with the next stitch to decrease back to 56 stitches. Continue working in the lace pattern as described above.

After 30 rounds of the lace pattern, switch to the rib pattern and work for another ¾" (1.9cm). Bind off loosely as you see fit.

Knitting Chart: Lace Pattern

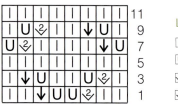

Legend
- I = K
- U = YO
- ⚡ = K2tog
- ↓ = SKP

42 THE LITTLE SOCK KNITTING BOOK

Size Chart for Toe-Up Sock

Gauge with 4-ply yarn and US size 1 ½–2 ½ (2.5–3mm) DPNs, knit in stockinette stitch: 28 stitches and 40 rows = 4" x 4" (10.2 x 10.2cm).

US Size (EU Size)	Kids' 6.5 (22)	Kids' 8 (24)	Kids' 9.5 (26)	Kids' 11.5 (29)	Kids' 12.5 (30)	Kids' 1.5 (33)	Women's 5 (35/36)	Women's 6.5 (37)	Women's 8 (38/39)	Women's 9.5 (40)	Men's 9.5 (42/43)	Men's 11 (44)	Men's 13 (46)	Men's 14 (47)
Sock length in inches (cm)	5 ¼" (13.3cm)	5 ¾" (14.6cm)	6 ¼" (15.9cm)	7" (17.8cm)	7 ½" (19.1cm)	8" (20.3cm)	8 ½" (21.6cm)	9" (22.9cm)	9 ⅔" (24.5cm)	10" (25.4cm)	10 ⅔" (27.1cm)	11" (27.9cm)	11 ½" (29.2cm)	12" (30.5cm)
Number of stitches for instep and sole	38	42	46	46	50	50	54	54	58	58	62	62	66	66
From toe to beginning of instep in inches (cm)	3 ⅛" (7.9cm)	3 ½" (8.9cm)	4 ⅛" (10.5cm)	4 ¾" (12.1cm)	5 ⅓" (13.5cm)	5 ¾" (14.6cm)	6 ⅛" (15.6cm)	6 ¾" (17.1cm)	7 ⅛" (18.1cm)	7 ½" (19.1cm)	7 ⅞" (20cm)	8 ¼" (21cm)	8 ⅔" (22cm)	9" (22.9cm)
Number of increases for instep and heel	3	3	4	4	5	5	6	6	7	7	8	8	9	9
Number of stitches for the heel flap	9	9	11	11	13	13	15	15	17	17	19	19	21	21
Number of decreases on the right and left of the heel flap	5	5	7	7	9	9	11	11	13	13	15	15	17	17
Number of stitches for the leg (lace cuff)	38	42	46	46	50	50	54	54	58	58	62	62	66	66

Knitting Basics

Knit (K)

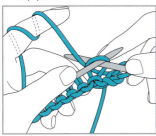

With the yarn behind the left needle, insert the right needle into the stitch from left to right, grab the yarn, and pull it through the stitch. Drop the stitch off the left needle.

Purl (P)

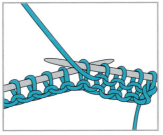

With the yarn in front of the left needle, insert the right needle from right to left into the stitch, wrap the yarn around the needle from front to back, and pull it through the stitch. Drop the stitch off the left needle.

Knit Through the Back Loop (Ktbl)

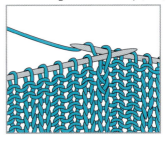

Insert the needle from front to back into the back loop of the stitch and knit as usual.

Right Lifted Increase (RLI)

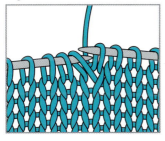

Insert the right needle into the following stitch of the row below and knit it. Then knit the stitch above it. The increase leans to the right.

Left Lifted Increase (LLI)

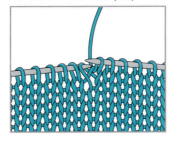

Knit 1 stitch, then with the left needle, pick up the loop of the stitch two rows below the one on the needle, and knit it. The increase leans to the left.

Make One Left (M1L)

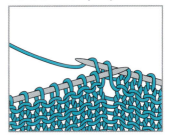

Pick up the bar between two stitches with the left needle from front to back, knit into the back of the loop, and let the bar slide off the left needle. This increase leans to the left.

Yarn Over (YO)

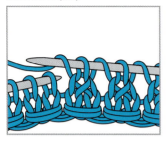

Bring the yarn from the front to the back over the right needle, and continue as directed.

Knit Two Together (K2tog)

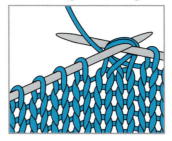

With the yarn behind the work, insert the right needle from left to right through both stitches, knit them together, and drop them off the left needle. The decrease leans to the right.

Slip One, Knit One, Pass Slipped Stitch Over (SKP)

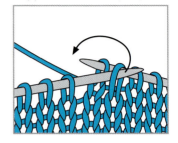

Slip 1 stitch knitwise, knit the next stitch, and pull the slipped stitch over it. The decrease leans to the left.

Purl Two Together (P2tog)

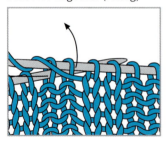

With the yarn in front of the work, insert the right needle from right to the left through both stitches, purl them together, and drop them off the left needle.

Knit Three Together (K3tog)

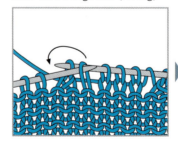

Slip the first stitch knitwise, then knit the next two stitches together.

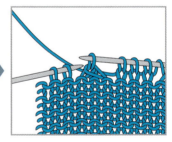

Pull the first slipped stitch over the two stitches that are knitted together.

Jacquard/Fair Isle Knitting

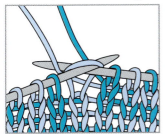

When knitting with multiple colors, carry the unused yarn loosely on the back side. When changing colors, slightly spread out the stitches on the right needle so the new yarn gets the proper spacing and the knitted fabric doesn't pull together.

3/3 Right Cross (Cable)

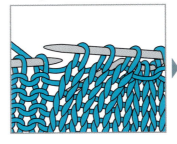

Place 3 stitches onto a cable needle and hold them behind the work. Knit the next 3 stitches from the left needle.

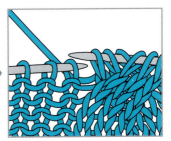

Now knit the 3 stitches from the cable needle. This creates a right-leaning twist or cable pattern.

Binding Off

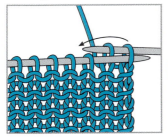

Knit the first two stitches. Using the left needle, pick up the first stitch and pull it over the second stitch to bind them off.

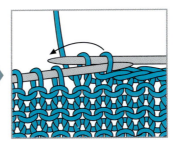

Knit the next stitch and repeat the process: pull the previous stitch over the current stitch. Once you've bound off all stitches, cut the yarn and pull it through the last stitch.

Weaving in Ends

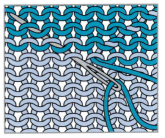

On the back side of the work, weave the yarn diagonally through the rows, always catching part of the stitch loops (not the entire loop).

The Little Sock Knitting Book

Landauer Publishing, www.landauerpub.com, is an imprint of Fox Chapel Publishing Company, Inc.

Copyright © 2025 by Fox Chapel Publishing Company, Inc.

© Christophorus Verlag in der Christian Verlag GmbH, Munich, Germany

The Little Sock Knitting Book is an translation of the 2024 version originally published in German by Christophorus Verlag under the title *Das kleine Sockenbuch* in Munich, Germany. This version is published by Landauer, an imprint of Fox Chapel Publishing Company, Inc.

All rights reserved. No part of this book may be reproduced, stored in a retrieval system, or transmitted in any form or by any means, electronic, mechanical, photocopying, recording, or otherwise, without the prior written permission of Fox Chapel Publishing, except for the inclusion of brief quotations in an acknowledged review.

Fox Chapel Publishing Team
Acquisitions Editor: Amelia Johanson
Translator: Freire. Diseño y comunicació, SL
Editor: Christa Oestreich
Designer: Freire. Diseño y comunicació, SL; Mike Deppen

Christophorus Verlag Team
Design and Realization: Kristin Benecken (30–31);
Veronika Hug (36–44); Simone Nägeli Pauli (34–35);
Birgit Rath-Israel (32–33)
Cover Design: Grafikwerk Freiburg
Photography: Rainer Muranyi (30–33, 36–44); Uwe Eberhard Schotte (34–35)

ISBN 978-1-63981-140-3

To learn more about the other great books from Fox Chapel Publishing, or to find a retailer near you, call toll-free at 800-457-9112 or visit us at www.FoxChapelPublishing.com.
You can also send mail to:
Fox Chapel Publishing
903 Square Street
Mount Joy, PA 17552

We are always looking for talented authors. To submit an idea, please send a brief inquiry to *acquisitions@foxchapelpublishing.com*.

Printed in China
Second printing

This book has been published with the intent to provide accurate and authoritative information in regard to the subject matter within. While every precaution has been taken in the preparation of this book, the author and publisher expressly disclaim any responsibility for any errors, omissions, or adverse effects arising from the use or application of the information contained herein.